How To Avoid Home Foreclosure

A Guide To Stopping Foreclosures

How To Avoid Home Foreclosure
A Guide To Stopping Foreclosures
by **Kelly Mailloux**

Printed in the United States of America

Copyright © 2010 **Kelly Mailloux**

Contents

Chapter 1

Introduction to foreclosure

There are a number of different events and situations that lead homeowners to the brink of foreclosure, including an unexpected job loss, or even a severe medical emergency. However, a number of other actions, even simply choosing the wrong type of loan when you purchase your home can also send you into similar dire financial territory.

If you should happen to take on a riskier loan, even if you do not have to pay a lot of

How To Avoid Home Foreclosure

money right from the start, you can find yourself facing foreclosure, especially if the interest rate on your loan is a variable rate meaning that it can go up when interest rates increase every year.

It does not really matter what the reasons are for your dire financial problems. What does matter is that all is not lost. There are options and alternatives available to you that are well worth trying. You still may be able to save your home, by filing for bankruptcy, or re negotiating your mortgage. If you want to try to save your home by avoiding foreclosure, then you will benefit from reading the entire book.

Keep in mind that avoiding foreclosure is no picnic. You will have to work hard, and be patient, but it is quite possible for many people to do so above all else: Do not give up.
Let's start with the basics and move on from there.

How To Avoid Home Foreclosure

What is a Mortgage? - - A mortgage is a type of loan, an the loan is used to purchase a piece of property. The property that is being purchased is treated like a guarantee for the amount of the loan. This guarantee acts as a lien against the property. Once you have signed all of the papers associated with the closing of the sale, the lien will be recorded in public records in the county court house. Until you pay the debt off and have the lien released, you cannot simply sell your home to someone else.

Even when a mortgage is in place and certain actions cannot be taken until the mortgage has been paid in full, you still have full ownership and full title to the property.

The lien being held against the mortgage does, however, give the lender the full right to sell off the secured property to recover his or her funds if you fail to make regular payments on the debt that you owe.

When applying for a mortgage, there are

How To Avoid Home Foreclosure

actually a number of different options available to you, including fixed rate mortgages, adjustable rate mortgages, balloon mortgages and interest only mortgages, just to name a few. For more information about these different types of mortgages, see the glossary at the end of this eBook.

Foreclosure is the process by which your lender can legally take ownership of your home from you, if you should happen to fail to hold up your end of the bargain detailed in your mortgage or deed of trust agreement. Once the lender forecloses upon your home, you have to move out otherwise you will be forcefully evicted.

In addition to losing ownership of your home, you can also lose a lot more. For example, you may still end up owing the lender more money, depending on the value of your home at the time of foreclosure. You will more than likely also destroy your credit rating in the

How To Avoid Home Foreclosure

process, which will make it much more difficult to buy a new home in the future.

There are two different types of foreclosure that you can find yourself facing: Judicial foreclosures, and non-judicial foreclosures. In either case, your property will more than likely be seized by the lender and put up for auction, and the highest bidder will become the new owner. In some cases the lender bids on the house during the auction, at whatever price the debt is owed at. If no other buyer bids higher than the lender, the lender wins the property and is able to turn a profit on your home and to get back all of the money that they lost in the transaction.

Pre foreclosure is the time period that exists between the day that the lender notifies you that a foreclosure lawsuit has been filed or the day that a Notice of Default has been filed, and the actual date that the property is slated to be sold at a public auction or in a trustee's

How To Avoid Home Foreclosure

sale. Just because you receive a notice like this, it simply does not mean that you have lost the fight. You still have the possibility of preventing a foreclosure from occurring.

For example, if you want to you can sell the property, or you may consider filing for bankruptcy. You may also consider refinancing, or devising a workout plan with your lender. The most important thing to understand is that all is not lost, and that you still can save your house.

The foreclosure rates are growing rapidly, and the number of homes being foreclosed upon in recent years has shot up significantly from the numbers a decade or two ago. You are not alone in this, and there are hundreds of thousands of other people all over the country who are fighting this same process at the exact same time.

Colorado, Illinois, Texas, Florida and California all experience some of the highest foreclosure percentages in the county. The state

How To Avoid Home Foreclosure

of Colorado experienced 68,310 foreclosures in 2006 alone. Illinois had 75,176 foreclosures in the same year. Texas, Florida and California saw steep increases in foreclosures, with 106,845, 120,989 and 157,417 respectively.

Do not become a statistic, by falling into this drastically growing number of foreclosures. Homeowners and families are not meant to be statistics. Now is your time to act, regardless of whether you are just falling into a debt problem, or have already received a foreclosure lawsuit notice, or a Notice of Default letter.

There is still time to save your home, your credit rating, and your financial situation, as long as you are willing to take the advice presented within these pages and to promise not to give up as long as you still have options and alternatives to explore.

Many people have managed to ward off foreclosure by re negotiating terms with a lender, by declaring bankruptcy, or by selling

How To Avoid Home Foreclosure

their homes on their own. There are options available to you, and all is not lost by any means.

Are you ready to figure out what your options are? The first thing that you need to understand is that not all opportunities out there are legitimate, and yes, there are unfortunately a lot of people out there who want to take advantage of you in your dire financial situation, so let us address foreclosure scams first before we begin to touch on the options available to you for avoiding foreclosure, surviving foreclosure and getting back on your feet after a foreclosure occurs.

Chapter 2

Foreclosure Scams

There are predators out there who look at homeowners in poor financial situations as easy prey, devising a number of scams and fraud attempts to take advantage of people who are already on a heck of a financial roller coaster. It is important that you protect yourself by staying current on the foreclosure fraud and scams that are circulating, so that you do not get taken by one of these fraudsters. Here are some of the more prevalent scams that people are trying to pull over on homeowners and families buying

How To Avoid Home Foreclosure

homes or facing foreclosure.

Sales Leaseback - People often tout this as an easy deal, requiring that the homeowner hand his or her deed over to an "investor" for little or no money, on the basis that the homeowner can continue to live in the home, leasing it back with the option of repurchasing within a year. This may sound like an excellent concept, but there is a serious catch involved.

Even if you sign the deed over to someone else, you are still legally responsible for the mortgage, meaning that you would be paying both the original mortgage and the lease amount to the investor. Paying twice what you were already having difficulty paying will be close to impossible and one missed or late payment will have you evicted from the home, and the home sold out from under you.

Predatory Lending - Unfortunately, there are a large number of lenders out there who offer loans with the specific intention of

How To Avoid Home Foreclosure

taking advantage of borrowers who cannot afford to make the payments. If there is any equity in the home at all, these lenders will attempt to take it all in the form of incredible fees, exorbitant interest rates, and nightmare prepayment penalties. While new laws are being passed that prohibit many of these predatory practices from occurring, it is still quite easy for lenders to take advantage of homeowners in bad financial situations.

Here are some of the predatory lending practices that you need to steer clear of:

Frequent Refinancing - The frequent refinancing of loans without offering any real benefits to the homeowner or borrower, or frequent refinancing of loans simply so that the lender may generate additional fees for him or herself.

Equity Switching - Equity stripping, by

persuading an owner in dire financial straights to take out a loan far beyond his or her ability to repay it.

Bait and Switch - Attempts at bait and switch, where lenders advertise a specific set of 'teaser' fees and interest rates, then the rates and fees skyrocket suddenly at the point of closing, reaching points that are beyond the homeowner's means.

Appraisal Inflation - Inflating appraisals up front, forcing the homeowner to take on much larger loans with much higher interest rates. Homeowners lose the opportunity to refinance the amount of the loan at a later time, because the value of the home is no longer enough to cover the full amount of the loan.

Loss Mitigation - This practice is regularly referred to as "I can prevent your foreclosure, but only if you pay a fee". People

How To Avoid Home Foreclosure

who try to force this type of a process on unsuspecting people tout it as the ability to stop or prevent foreclosure, but only for a fee paid up front. The problem with this type of service is that the "rescuer" cannot guarantee that they will actually prevent your foreclosure from occurring, yet they still collect your fee up front. If you want to protect yourself as a homeowner in a bad financial situation, there are much easier ways to do it without paying exorbitant fees to "rescuers" who more than likely will not be able to help you.

List and Sell - This is a scheme that is becoming quite popular among real estate agents and brokers looking for additional income streams. The concept is simple: The real estate agent convinces a homeowner in default to allow the agent to list the home in an attempt to sell it. The real estate agent promises that if the home is not sold within the period before the foreclosure auction, which is

How To Avoid Home Foreclosure

typically around sixty days away, he or she will purchase it.

But here is the catch: In too many cases, the real estate agent will drastically overprice the property when listing it in the MLS or Multiple Listing Service, so that nobody expresses any interest in purchasing it. Then when it does not sell, the agent is able to purchase it for substantially less than what it was listed for.

Hiding things in the contract - Some scammers and predatory lenders like to hide a variety of different bombshells right in the contract where they cannot be found. They wait until the absolute last minute, and then make these hidden terms known. By now, it is too late for the homeowner to renegotiate the contract, and he or she is trapped dealing with the true intentions of the contract.

Homeowners who are caught in situations like these are very rarely capable of seeking

How To Avoid Home Foreclosure

legal advice. They suddenly find out that there are costs behind their resources, but if they fight the contract at closing they could potentially lose their home in the foreclosure process.

There are a number of organizations, like ACORN or the Association of Community Organizations for Reform Now, the Consumer's Union, and the United States Office of Housing and Urban Development or HUD that offer extremely vital and valuable insight into protecting yourself from predatory lending practices and everything that is well within your power to combat these dangerous practices.

For more information on protecting yourself from predatory lending practices and other fraud and scam attempts, you can find the links to these organizations in the resources section at the end of this eBook.

How To Avoid Home Foreclosure

Chapter 3

Protect Yourself From Foreclosure

As we mentioned before, all is not lost when it comes to protecting yourself from foreclosure. Here are the steps that you need to follow to protect yourself from the foreclosure process. Keep in mind that once your lender has expressed his or her plans to foreclose on your home, your time is extremely limited. This is a fast moving process, and because time is of the essence, you have to act fast if you want to

How To Avoid Home Foreclosure

succeed.

1 - For starters, do not ignore the problem. As you become further and further behind in your finances, the more difficult it will become for you to reinstate your mortgage loan. The harder it becomes to reinstate your mortgage loan, the more easily your lender will find it to take your home from you.

2 - Contact your lender as soon as you know that there is a problem. Nothing dictates that you have to wait until your lender plans to foreclose. In reality, lenders do not want your home; they would rather you simply paid your mortgage on time so that they can be paid back for their investment. Because of this, most lenders offer options to help borrowers through a number of different financial difficulties.

3 - Keep in touch with your lender in every step of the process. Open and respond to any and all mail from your lender, because the first notices that you receive will offer a lot of

How To Avoid Home Foreclosure

vital information regarding the foreclosure prevention process. By failing to keep in touch and to open the mail that your lender sends simply will not be a good enough excuse when you finally end up in foreclosure court.

4 - Know your rights and your options when it comes to foreclosure. You can find a lot of valuable information relating to foreclosure prevention or loss mitigation online. Make sure that you know your rights, as informed decision making is the best way to prepare yourself for this challenging process.

5 - Use your assets to the best of your ability. Do you have assets like jewelry, a second vehicle, a whole life insurance policy, or other types of assets that you can use to sell for cash? Selling items that you can bear to part with will allow you to reinstate your loan. Using your assets to the best of your ability can have a huge impact on your ability to repay your mortgage and to save your home.

How To Avoid Home Foreclosure

6 - Avoid companies that charge money to do what you can do yourself. You should never have to pay exorbitant fees for help with foreclosure prevention. Use that money to pay your mortgage off instead. For profit companies will contact you with a variety of wild claims regarding negotiating with your lender, but they are doing this hoping that you do not realize that you can negotiate with your lender all on your own without their help and overpriced services.

These may be legitimate companies, but there is nothing that they do that you cannot do yourself, and your lender would more than likely rather hear from you than a professional company when it comes to *your* mortgage loan.

There are a variety of options available to you that do not require you to lose your home. With so many alternatives, it seems ludicrous that so many people find themselves losing their properties to a completely avoidable

Re-Negotiating the Loan - This option would allow you to use the equity that you have already established in your home as a way to pay off the delinquent amount in your current mortgage loan. Your monthly payments may even be reduced, but this depends on the interest rate of your new loan.

Modifying the Terms of the Loan - An option like this will allow you to refinance the debt in your mortgage, or even to extend the current term of your existing mortgage loan. Modifications are changes that are made to a mortgage loan without having to refinance.

Developing a Workout Plan - Developing a repayment plan typically involves establishing a new schedule that allows you to make full regular monthly payment plans to your lender plus a little bit of extra money every month so that you can repay the delinquent

How To Avoid Home Foreclosure

amount that you owe over a pre determined amount of time.

Forbearance - Special forbearance plan options may give you a temporary reduction or a temporary suspension of your monthly mortgage payments, based on the lender's ability to later increase your payments at a point where you are more financially stable. The increase in your payments will cover the delinquent amount that was accrued, but over a longer period of time than simply demanding payment in full.

There are also options available that allow you to dispose of your home to avoid the foreclosure process all together. While losing your home all together is not always an ideal situation, it is a viable option and therefore is well worth exploring.

In situations where you do not have interest in retaining ownership of your home, the following disposition options may be

How To Avoid Home Foreclosure

available to you as alternatives to the foreclosure process. These options will affect your credit rating a lot less than the foreclosure process would.

- **Sell the Home** - If there is a sufficient amount of equity in the property, you could actually receive more for the property than what is currently due on the mortgage loan, allowing you to pay the mortgage off and to walk away with some cash in your pocket as well.

- **Assumption** - Using this option, what you would do is to sign the property over to another person who would take over the possession of your home, and would handle making the payments from that moment forward.

- **Pre-Foreclosure Sale** - This option, which

How To Avoid Home Foreclosure

we will touch on more in the next
chapter, will allow you to sell your
property for less than what is necessary
to pay for your mortgage loan.

- **Deed in Lieu of Foreclosure** - This option
may allow you to "give back" the
property to your lender voluntarily,
without damaging your credit further
than you already have.

If you do decide to sell your home, because
time is of the essence in the foreclosure
process, you need to be quick about it. While
you may not necessarily fetch a lot of money
for the property, to avoid foreclosure it is
important to accept what you are offered in
many cases.

Your luck in this situation may lay in the fact
that there are many savvy investors out there
who are looking to buy properties for decent

How To Avoid Home Foreclosure

amounts of money in the pre foreclosure and foreclosure phases. Homes that have been defaulted on still often have equity in them, and this equity can be extremely valuable to the right investors.

If you are having difficultly working with a real estate agent that has what it takes to quickly sell your home, you may want to start looking for investors who pay cash for homes that have been defaulted on or pushed into the pre foreclosure phase.

While it is not a good idea to have to give your home up, in some circumstances the only way to protect yourself from foreclosure is to pay the entire mortgage loan off quickly by unloading your house to the first investor who offers you a good deal. If you wait and the lender takes your home, you will get far less for it than you deserve and may still end up owing money to the lender.

How To Avoid Home Foreclosure

Chapter 4

Pre-foreclosure

The pre foreclosure period is the period that exists from the day that your lender notifies you of his or her intention to foreclosure, and the date that is set for the public sale of your home. There are a couple of different options available for you to explore at this point, one of which is to pursue a short sale, one of which is a Deed in Lieu of

How To Avoid Home Foreclosure

foreclosure opportunity, and the final of which is to talk to someone regarding bankruptcy proceedings.

All three of these situations fit certain circumstances and situations, and not every will qualify. Find out more information about these strategies to see if any of the three is right for your unique circumstances.

Short Selling - When it comes to real estate, a short sale occurs when the outstanding obligations against a property have become greater than what the property is capable of selling for. The short sale process is a way that homeowners can avoid having their homes foreclosed upon while still paying their loan off by settling with the mortgage lender.

The first step is to verify what the value is for your property, through a real estate broker or through your own market analysis of your property and the surrounding area. Next you will add up all of the costs associated with

How To Avoid Home Foreclosure

selling the property, and the amount that is owed against the property which will be the total of all of the loans currently against the property. You will need to do some calculating, subtracting the total amount owed against the property from the estimated sale proceeds. On a short sale, the number that you come up with will be a negative one.

Your next step is to directly contact each lender, talking to someone in the customer service department and explaining the situation to them in detail. They may either recommend you talk to a specific department, or they may put you in touch with the right supervisor or manager right away. The more authority this person has, the better.

Talk to your lender at this point to find out more about what is required for a short sale. Most but not all lenders will be more than willing to work with you, reducing how much money is left on your loan, or making other

How To Avoid Home Foreclosure

arrangements for you to follow.

Keep in mind that closing costs tend to include both title and escrow fees, and you may be responsible for these as the seller of the property but it depends on your county. You may also have to deal with notary fees, re conveyance fees, documentary fees, transfer fees, delivery fees, unpaid property taxes and attorney fees as well.

You also need to keep in mind if you do not use the assistance of a real estate broker when you sell the home, you can save the commission amount and apply it toward your loan instead. But if you feel more secure having a real estate broker, you should consider working with a discount broker who can market your property more cheaply.

Deed in Lieu of Foreclosure - This is a deed instrument that allows the borrower to convey all of the interest in a piece of real estate property to the lender as a means of

How To Avoid Home Foreclosure

satisfying the loan in default and avoiding foreclosure proceedings in the process. This specific process offers a number of advantages both to the lender and to the borrower.

The principal advantage offered to the borrower is that he or she is immediately released from most or all of the debt associated with the loan that has been defaulted on. The borrower is also able to avoid the public notoriety that comes with a formal foreclosure. The lender can enjoy a large reduction in the amount of time and cost that would normally be associated with a home repossession, along with other advantages should the borrower subsequently file for bankruptcy proceedings.

In order for a borrower to even be considered for a deed in lieu of foreclosure, the amount of debt must be secured by the transfer of the real estate. Both parties in the transaction must enter in to the agreement in good faith and voluntarily. What this does, is it

How To Avoid Home Foreclosure

enacts the parole evidence rule, protecting the
lender from subsequent claims that he or she
acted in bad faith or otherwise pressured the
borrower into this type of settlement.

Chapter 5

Surviving A Foreclosure

As long as you are willing to be open and honest with your lender, and you are not afraid to set up some kind of payment arrangement that you can actually commit to; the odds are that your lender will be willing to work with you, allowing you to avoid the foreclosure process all together. If you want to stop or overturn the foreclosure process, something has to be

How To Avoid Home Foreclosure

legitimately wrong with the process, and this is not simple.

So instead of simply fighting off foreclosure, you can prevent it completely by making the right monthly payments every month. As we mentioned, there are plenty of alternative options to try if you want to put off the foreclosure process or to stop it all together.

If the sale of your home does take place, try not to fret. You probably still have time to move on to another home before the paperwork has been completely finalized.

When your credit is severely damaged already and then you are forced into the foreclosure process, you will find it even more difficulty to avoid this from happening, especially if you simply do not have the resources necessary to completely avoid a foreclosure. You may not be able to see into the future, but any precautions that you can take to avoid the foreclosure process should be taken

How To Avoid Home Foreclosure

as soon as possible. Foreclosures are occurring at truly record rates, and families and home owners are constantly facing obstacles forcing them to forfeit their ability to make payments on their property mortgages.

After you receive a foreclosure notification, you should call your lender immediately and set up an appointment where you can meet with them in person. Sit down with them individually and try to find out if there is anything that you can do to stop the foreclosure process from occurring. There are new laws that require that credit counseling be offered to debtors from approved non-profit credit advisory companies, hoping to drastically decrease how many people are experiencing foreclosures every year.

As long as you do not owe more money than what your home will sell for in the current real estate market, then selling your home may even give you the profit that you are looking for

How To Avoid Home Foreclosure

before your home goes into foreclosure. The key here is to thoroughly explore your options.

You absolutely need to be prepared if you want to survive foreclosure. Try everything that you can first to prevent it from occurring, but know that if you cannot prevent foreclosure, it is not the end of the world. Talk to your lender through every step of the process and see what he or she can do for you as you go along through step by step. Your lender may be able to help you a lot more than you realize.

Chapter 6

Restore Credit Following Foreclosure

Losing your home is one of the absolute worst things that can ever happen to most people. Foreclosure is an ugly word, and most people do not want to think about it. What most people do not know, or refuse to believe is that you can recover after a foreclosure, and the sooner you start working at it, the better off you will be.

You simply have to know what to do and how to do it to protect yourself and to begin building your credit back up again. Rebuilding

How To Avoid Home Foreclosure

your credit after you have experienced a foreclosure can be a tricky proposition. This is a simple step by step formula for restoring your credit after you lose your home in the foreclosure process.

-   **Step 1** - First thing you need to do is to understand why you were foreclosed on. This is an absolutely vital and extremely important factor in repairing your credit following a foreclosure. Were there circumstances that you could have avoided? If so, you need to understand what they were so that in the future, you can fix them or avoid them all together. If it was simply a series of unfortunately accidents and circumstances beyond your control, do what you can to prevent them from reoccurring.

- **Step 2** - The next step in the process is to look into how you spend your money. Your

38

How To Avoid Home Foreclosure

personal spending habits may need to see some change so that you can avoid having this same type of problem again in the future.

You need to create a personal budget for yourself, and you need to stick to it at all costs so that you can correct the bad ways that you spend your money. Your goal here is to save some money so that you can better avoid falling into such a negative situation ever again.

- **Step 3** - Your next step in this process is to pay off all of your debts. This is not going to be an easy task for most people, not by any means, especially if you have a number of different debts to pay off.

However, there are a number of innovative debt consolidation services that are well worth you considering. Just make sure that you do your research and really check out your options

How To Avoid Home Foreclosure

because not all debt consolidation companies are created equally, and some companies are fraudulent.

- **Step 4** - Now your job is to maintain your spending habits. It can be fairly easy for people to fall back into their old habits, the same habits that got them into the foreclosure mess to begin with. Because of this, it is imperative that you be committed to the act of changing.

One of the best ways to make sure that this happens is to cut up your credit cards, this way you cannot be tempted to use them again, especially in the worst possible situations. Getting into debt simply to pay off other debt is absolutely NOT the way that you should handle things.

- **Step 5** - The final step to build your credit up again after a foreclosure is to make sure that

How To Avoid Home Foreclosure

from this point on, you pay everything off on time. This will help you repair your credit step by step after your foreclosure. You need to be willing to make sacrifices if you want to get your bills paid up on time. The more that you show that you have changed, the more quickly you will be able to repair your credit.

How To Avoid Home Foreclosure

Chapter 7

Foreclosure Glossary

Adjustable Rate Mortgage - These are also known as ARMs, and are mortgages that have interest rates that change on a periodic basis. The interest rate is generally pegged to some standard rate when you take this type of loan.

Appraisal - This is a written justification that explains the price that is paid for a specific property. The appraisal is typically based on the analysis of other similar homes that are in the nearby area, or on comparable sales within the community.

Asset - Assets are items that have value and that are owned by a single individual. There are a variety of different types of assets that can be converted directly into cash. These assets are referred to as liquid assets because they can be easily liquefied into cash. Liquid assets include banking accounts, bonds, stocks, mutual funds and many others. Other types of assets include personal property, real estate and debts that are owned to an individual by other individuals.

Assumes and Agrees to Pay - this is a clause that can be found in a number of different types of deeds and related documents, and it states that when the buyer decides to take over the payments that originally belonged to a seller's old mortgage loan, he or she is also agreeing to pay off the old loan in its entirety. The buyer is normally responsible for obtaining the title and

How To Avoid Home Foreclosure

then making whatever payments should happen to follow. You can usually find this clause in the section of the document pertaining to the transfer of the title of the property to the buyer from the seller. This clause may or may not completely release the seller from any and all liabilities.

Balloon Mortgage - A balloon mortgage is a mortgage where you pay an agreed upon interest rate on the loan, but only for a pre specified amount of time. At the end of this pre determined time period, the total amount of the mortgage becomes due. This is a viable lending option for some people, but those facing foreclosure are probably better off not exploring this particular option.

Bankruptcy - After filing in a federal court for bankruptcy proceedings, individuals can either relieve or restructure their liabilities and their debts through the bankruptcy process. There are actually a number of different types of bankruptcies, but the most prevalent are Chapter 7 Bankruptcy which is no asset bankruptcy, and Chapter 13 bankruptcy.

Chapter 7 bankruptcy is capable of relieving most types of debt that the borrower is facing. Borrowers cannot generally become qualified for paper loans for at least two years after the bankruptcy is discharged, and people are required to re establish their ability to repay debt, meaning that they need to build their credit up again before they will qualify for a mortgage loan.

Chapter 7 - This is a chapter in the Federal Bankruptcy Code that calls for liquidation. What this means, is that any assets that are belonging to the debtor that are non exempt will be given up, or sold off for the benefit of whatever creditors are still owed money, in the order of their priority.

In Chapter 7 bankruptcy, the debt is never actually discharged. Secured creditors need to continue to receive their payments or assets to pay off the loans that they are still owed, while unsecured creditors receive very little if anything in return for their loans when Chapter 7 bankruptcy is filed.

Chapter 13 - This is a chapter of the Federal Bankruptcy Code giving wage earners the ability to reduce debt through court orders according to planned terms that allow debtors to pay much of the original amounts owed if not the total amount owed.

Deed in Lieu - This option may allow you to "give back" the property to your lender voluntarily, without damaging your credit further than you already have. Lenders can decide from this point whether they want to cease the foreclosure activity if the borrower asks to provide this option.

Deed of Trust - In nearly half of all of the United States, deeds of trust are used rather than mortgages. However, just like mortgages, deeds of trust are recorded in public records so that everyone will know that a lien is placed on your property.

Three parties are involved in the deed of trust: You are the trustor, as the homeowner who took the loan out, then there is a beneficiary, which is the financial institution providing the money for the loan, and finally there is a neutral third party known as the trustee.

Equity - This is a home owner's financial interest in a particular piece of property. Equity is calculated as the real difference that exists

How To Avoid Home Foreclosure

between the fair market value on a property, and the amount of money that is still owned on its mortgage loan, and on any other liens that are attached to it.

Fixed Rate Mortgage - This is a mortgage where the interest rate is set when you first take the loan, and then it remains the same throughout the entire length of the loan.

Forbearance - This occurs when the lender voluntarily accepts to take lower payments than what was originally agreed to in the documents for the loan, but only for a specific period of time so that the borrower can recover financially from a job loss or some other financial issue.

Foreclosure - Foreclosure is defined as the local process or processes by which a borrower who has defaulted on a mortgage loan is deprived of their ownership rights to the mortgaged property. What this typically involves is the forced sale of the property at a trustee's sale or public auction. The proceeds of the sale are then applied to the debt that has been accrued by the mortgage.

Interest Only Mortgage - These are mortgages where you only pay the interest portion of the loan, and your payment does not include any part of the principal portion of the mortgage loan.

Lender - This is a term that refers to the institutions that make loans, along with any other individuals that represent the firm that makes the loan. Loan officers and lending companies are both commonly referred to as lenders.

Lien - Liens are defined as legal claims that are

made against properties. Liens need to be paid off completely in full any time that the property is sold. Mortgages and first trust needs are normally considered to be liens.

Mortgage - A mortgage is a type of loan, and the loan is used to purchase a piece of property. The property that is being purchased is treated like a guarantee for the amount of the loan. This guarantee acts as a lien against the property.

Principal - The principal part of the loan is the amount that is borrowed, or rather the amount that was borrowed but that still remains unpaid. The principal is also regarded as the part of a monthly payment that actually reduces the balance of the mortgage that is actually still remaining to be paid, not including the interest rate or the interest that was accrued.

How To Avoid Home Foreclosure

Real Estate Agent - A real estate agent is a person who has obtained the proper licensing to negotiate and to transact in all of the steps that are normally associated with selling real estate property. Real estate agents can deal in residential property, commercial property or a combination of the two.

Real Property - In essence, the concept of "real property" falls into the scope of any items that have tangible ownership capability. This includes land, and including anything that has a permanent nature like rocks, landscaping, trees, and structures and so on.

Realtor - Realtors are real estate agents, real estate associations, real estate associates and real estate brokers who hold an active membership in one or more of any local real estate boards. The real estate board has to be accredited and affiliated with the National

How To Avoid Home Foreclosure

Association of Realtors to qualify.

Second Mortgage - Second mortgages are mortgages that have lean positions that act as subordinate mortgages to the first mortgage. Second mortgages can be used either to reduce or to improve the terms of the first mortgage, or to draw an amount of cash out of the original mortgage based in the form of equity in the home. When it comes to foreclosure proceedings, the lender with the first mortgage always has precedence over the lender dealing with the second mortgage.

Short Sale - This is a specific type of workout procedure that involves the lender accepting less than the full balance due on the loan. This is an option made available to homeowners who want to sell their home quickly and for less than the fair market value of the property in order to avoid the proceedings dealing with foreclosure.

How To Avoid Home Foreclosure

Title - The title is a legal document that exists to clearly evidence a person's right to the express ownership of a piece of property. Titles are most commonly used for vehicles and properties.

Two Step Mortgage - Two step mortgages are adjustable rate mortgages, or ARM mortgages that have a single interest rate for the first five or seven years of length for the mortgage term, and then the interest rate changes for the remainder of the amortization term of the mortgage to reflect a different interest rate all together. The two very different mortgage rates are what make this a "two step" mortgage.

Wage Earner's Plan - The Wage Earner's Plan is just another nickname for the Chapter 13 division of bankruptcy proceedings.

Warranty Deed - A warranty deed is a

How To Avoid Home Foreclosure

conveyance of land, and involves the grantor guaranteeing the title of the land to the grantee.

Without Recourse - These are words that are most commonly used in the process of endorsing either a note or a bill. The note or bill is endorsed to denote that the future holder of a piece of property is not allowed to turn to the endorser in the event that there is a issue with making payment on time.

Workout - A workout is a process by which a borrower or home owner comes to a mutually acceptable arrangement on a financial basis with the lender of a deed or mortgage as a means of avoiding a foreclosure on the horizon. Not all lenders offer workout plans, but many are more than willing to help borrowers overcome their financial issues to avoid foreclosure.

How To Avoid Home Foreclosure

Wrap Around - This is a specific type of mortgage that involves the obligation to pay later liens including the obligation to also pay earlier lien mortgages at the same time. Essentially speaking, the later mortgage is wrapped around the earlier mortgage, and any defaults that are placed on the earlier lien or mortgage are automatically defaulted on the later lien mortgages as well.

Wrap Around Loan - A wrap around loan is a newer type of loan, and it encompasses any and all existing loans, passing defaults from older loans onto the new loans in the process.

Wrongful Foreclosure - This is a type of foreclosure that in some way or another was legally improper. Wrongful foreclosure is a foreclosure that caused a borrower to needlessly suffer wrongful and purely unnecessary damages.

Chapter 8

Resources

The right resources can be what prevents a homeowner from losing their home to foreclosure, and the difference between an easily preventable situation and serious hardship. Arm yourself with the right tools, resources and information and you can prevent foreclosure from occurring simply by exercising the variety of other options that are available to you.

Organization Resources

ACORN, the Association of Community Organizations for Reform Now, which can be found at http://www.acorn.org.

The Consumers Union, which can be found at http://www.consumersunion.org.

HUD, The United States Office of Housing and Urban Development, which can be found at http://www.hud.gov/buying/localpredlend.cfm.

Book Resources

"The 250 Questions you should ask to Avoid Foreclosure" - by Lita Epstein - Not only is this an invaluable resource for families

How To Avoid Home Foreclosure

facing foreclosure, but it also has a comprehensive chapter on all of the different laws and regulations that matter in different states. If you need to know what laws and regulations are specific to your state when it comes to foreclosure, picking this book up is absolutely vital.

"The Survival Guide to Foreclosure" - by Clyde Goulet - This is another vital guide to preventing foreclosure, offering all of the information that you need to know to survive a foreclosure, to restore your credit, and to restore your home ownership ability.

How To Avoid Home Foreclosure

Website Resources

http://www.hud.gov/foreclosure/index.cfm

http://homebuying.about.com/od/4closuresh
ortsales/qt/011708_stopfore.htm

http://www.freddiemac.com/corporate/buyo
wn/english/avoiding_foreclosure/

http://portal.hud.gov/portal/page?
pageid=33,717348&_dad=portal&_schema=
PORTAL

http://www.mortgage101.com/Articles/Bank
ruptcy.asp?ArticleID=1137&p=mtg101
http://www.ehow.com/how_7235_avoid-
foreclosure.html

http://www.businessweek.com/bwdaily/dnfl
ash/content/feb2007/db20070205_724704.h
tm

How To Avoid Home Foreclosure

http://bankruptcy.lawyers.com/foreclosures/
Real-Estate-How-to-Avoid-Foreclosure-
FAQs.html

http://www.debtworkout.com/foreclosuresto
p10.html

http://www.americanloansearch.com/info-
foreclosure.htm

How To Avoid Home Foreclosure